MW00624826

HOW TO SELF-PUBLISH YOUR BOOK

HOW TO SELF-PUBLISH YOUR BOOK

A PRACTICAL GUIDE TO CREATING AND DISTRIBUTING YOUR E-BOOK OR PRINT BOOK

CARLA KING

PBS MediaShift
San Francisco

How to Self-Publish Your Book Copyright © 2013 by PBS MediaShift.

This book was produced using PressBooks.com, and PDF rendering was done by PrinceXML.

Contents

Introduction: There's No Stopping You Now

For over a decade my self-publishing audiences were filled with dejected, rejected authors. But in the last few years, new faces appeared in the crowd: traditionally published authors, literary agents, editors and publishers. Why? Self-published books finally reached the mainstream, with enough success stories to make self-publishers legitimate citizens of the book world. So what happened? E-reading devices became popular, print book and e-book creation tools became easy to use, social media made marketing easier, traditional publishers lost revenue and stopped paying living wages, new companies based on new technologies gave authors spectacularly better royalties, and traditionally published authors jumped ship.

Whether you are self-publishing a personal book, or you are dedicated to self-publishing as a business, or you want to attract a publishing partner, you can now do it yourself cheaply, easily and proudly. Plot your success by choosing the reputable tools and services recommended here, along with techniques that will help your book succeed in the market that you choose.

PART I

The Basics: Tools and Services

1

Recommended Tools and Services: The Short List

Among the hundreds of self-publishing tools and services are an outstanding few. The vendors on this short list were chosen for their ease-of-use, reliability, reputation, innovation, evolving feature set, fair pricing and dedication to the advancement of the self-publishing author.

Many of these are do-it-yourself tools and some are full-service. Some offer you the option to hand over your files and a few hundred bucks to have the conversion and distribution done for you. It can't get much easier than that.

E-Book Creation and Distribution

- **Smashwords** is the largest distributor of indie e-books, delivering to e-book retailers, app stores, and libraries. The e-book conversion and publishing service is free, and they take a 15% commission on sales. Upload your properly-formatted Word document under 5MB in size, or upload your own custom-designed EPUB file. Their cool Coupon Generator feature makes custom promotions a snap.
- **Amazon Kindle Direct Publishing** (KDP) distributes your properly-formatted e-book to the Amazon Kindle store, the only place Smashwords does not distribute. You can either create it yourself using a Word doc or other supported file format (just make a few changes to the Smashwords edition) or, if you've made a print-on-demand book with CreateSpace, pay just $65 to order up a perfectly formatted KDP file for the Kindle version.

- **BookBaby** is a complete e-book publishing and distribution service. Hand over your files for conversion from any format (including images and multimedia). They pass on 100% of net sales to authors. Packages run from $99 to $249, with an annual $19 fee after the second year. BookBaby also offers high-quality short-run printing, web hosting and cover design.
- **Vook** is an e-book creation and distribution service that can format plain-text e-books, picture e-books, and multimedia e-books for you. After conversion, you can request to use their browser-based tool to finesse or edit your book, and they have good cover design and editing services. They charge a 15% commision on sales, and their e-commerce platform Stripe takes 2.9% and charges a $0.30 per transaction fee.
- **Aerbook Maker**'s strength is in creating sophisticated picture and multimedia e-books. They provide a browser-based (cloud) e-book builder where you can experiment for free, and pay $99 for five formats when you're ready export your files. Do it yourself or they'll help you for a reasonable fee. You get the files to distribute as you wish.
- **Kwik** is a Photoshop plug-in for creating interactive books and even games for $249. People who love Photoshop love Kwik. You get the files to distribute as you wish. (They'll help you for a reasonable fee.)
- **Scrivener** is a word processing program with e-book and print book formatting capability. Lots of writers use it to develop and organize their books, scripts and even articles. You have the files so you can send the PDF to a printer, and distribute the e-book files as you wish.
- **PressBooks** is a browser-based publishing system based on the WordPress blogging and content management platform. It's 100% free to use and publish in e-book and print formats, with paid premium features including premium themes. They will help you for a reasonable fee. They promote BookBaby's e-book distribution service, but you have the print and e-book formatted files to distribute as you wish.

- **Folium Book Studio** is a cloud-based service that lets you create plain-text, image-heavy e-books and multimedia, including cover. Experiment for free, and when you're ready to publish, pay about $40. FBS exports multiple EPUB, HTML, and Kindle formats, They also offer full-service book building, cover design services, and fixed-format for Apple iPad. You get the files to distribute as you wish.
- **eBook Architects** is a very high-quality e-book conversion service that makes your book look great in all the popular formats, even very highly formatted e-books with images, footnotes, lists, sidebars, pull quotes, indexes, glossaries, foreign languages, special symbols, math, multiple columns, complex page design, script/screenplay formatting, poetry, tables, and other formatting. They can also scan your print book and convert it to a Word document for proofreading before e-book conversion. The average plain-text e-book conversion costs about $200, with add-on fees of $1-$4 per page or $100 per hour for more complex formatting. Turnaround time can be up to 6 weeks. You get the files to distribute as you wish.
- **Leanpub** is both a publishing and sales tool that outputs to PDF, EPUB, and Kindle formats, and they have an online store which specializes in selling in-progress e-books. If you're familiar with Dropbox and comfortable editing plain-text files (you'll use their "Markdown" formatting) in Notepad or TextEdit, you'll probably like it a lot. You can set minimum and suggested prices for your book, and readers can pay what they want using sliders. It's free to create your book, and you earn 90% minus 50 cents per sale.
- **KindleGen** is a free conversion tool that creates KF8 and Mobi (Kindle) formatted files from your EPUB, HTML and other file types so your book can be read by Kindle devices. It's a free download from Amazon, and easy to use. Once converted, you can upload your book to the KDP program for sale in the Kindle store.

Print On Demand (POD) Creation and Distribution

- **Amazon CreateSpace** is both a do-it-yourself and full-service print-on-demand service that lets you create and distribute your black and white or color print book to Amazon and the other retailers. Use their free interior and cover templates or, if you want professional help, they offer a variety of services from design to copyediting to marketing. Once it's finished, they'll convert it to Kindle format for $65. Royalty is 40% to 80% depending on the sales channel.

- **Lightning Source** (LSI) is Ingram Content Group's publisher services company with an extremely far-reaching print book distribution network that lets you set your bookstore (retailer) discount to 55% so bookstores may actually order it. Most self-publishers, however, since they won't be stocked on bookstore shelves, find it adequate to use CreateSpace instead.

Sales and Distribution Services

- **PigeonLab** distributes your e-books, including enhanced e-books, to markets worldwide, and they also specialize in getting overseas authors into US bookstores. Hand them your already-formatted e-book files (from eBook Architects, PressBooks, Scrivener, Folium Studio, or similar) and they'll do it all for you. Check sales reports, royalty payments and more with their author dashboard. They charge 10% of sales for their services.
- **Gumroad** is an online store. Upload and sell your digital files, up to 4 GB – or create an order form so you can sell physical objects. Automatically share your item with your Twitter and Facebook networks. Set a firm price or let the customer choose with pay-what-you-want pricing. You get the customer's email address. Royalty is 95% minus a 25-cent transaction free.
- **Leanpub**, described above, is an online store as well as an book creation tool.

As mentioned in the beginning of this chapter, these are by no means the only good tools and services available today, and new companies are popping up all the time. A good practice for deciding who to work with is to compare similar products with the companies on this list with features, services and pricing. For example, all of these services range from $0 to $300 for the typical book, or charge 10 or 15% on net. So this is your first tip – if a self-publishing service charges for "packages" that cost more than that, and many do, the red flag should go up. To illustrate, I've described some of the difficulties authors have had when using some of the all-inclusive self-publishing packages in the next chapter.

2

The Pitfalls of Using Self-Publishing Packages

On the surface, buying a self-publishing package seems much easier than finding and hiring a half-dozen professionals to create your book. But is it worth it? The short answer is no, which is why I tracked the reputable and affordable services named in the previous chapter.

Just in case you're still tempted, this chapter explores some of the potential danger zones of working with some services, as exposed by authors who were seduced by the promises of quick and easy self-publishing packages. I also offer some advice about avoiding these pitfalls — which can largely be avoided by using reputable tools and services described elsewhere in this book.

Self-Publishing Packages

Author Solutions (ASI) owns Author House, Booktango, Inkubook, iUniverse, Trafford, Xlibris, Wordclay, AuthorHive, Pallbrio, and Hollywood Pitch, all "self-publishing" companies that offer varying self-publishing "packages." ASI is owned by Penguin, which was bought by Pearson, which was, in turn, acquired by Random House. Even before these mergers, ASI spent a lot of money on marketing and their advertising dominates in Google ads on web pages that have anything to do with self-publishing. ASI also runs the self-publishing engine of Harlequin (DellArte), Hay House (Balboa), Thomas Nelson (West Bow) and other publishers who see their business shrinking as the self-publishing industry booms.

Let's compare ASI's Booktango with a couple of the providers recommended in this book:

- Booktango's e-book packages range from free to $359, with add-on's such as a $2999 social media service, $1799 book video service, and $599 Hollywood coverage, to name just a few.
- Smashwords is free, giving authors 85% of earnings. Smashwords doesn't sell anything but the authors' e-books, and almost reluctantly passes on an email list of e-book formatters and cover designers you can negotiate with yourself. Smashwords also provides a free *E-book Marketing Guide* and *Secrets to E-book Publishing Success*.
- BookBaby makes its money by signing up authors for $99 to $249. BookBaby, whose premium publishing e-book packages top out at $249, sells add-on services like design and formatting, with fees topping out at $279.
- Amazon KDP gives the author 70% of earnings, and Amazon CreateSpace (print) 80%. Their KDP Select marketing program costs nothing but temporary exclusive rights to your e-book.

Smashwords founder Mark Coker is a longtime critic of Author Solutions, pointing out in his blog that they make more money from selling services to authors than selling authors' books: "Author Solutions is one of the companies that put the 'V' in vanity. Author Solutions earns two-thirds or more of their income selling services and books to authors, not selling authors' books to readers," Coker writes.

Writing and publishing blogger Jane Friedman, in her popular Writer Unboxed blog, notes that ASI's packages are "incredibly overpriced when compared to the new and growing competition, and has less to recommend it with each passing day, as more success stories come from the e-publishing realm where author royalties are in the 70-85% range."

Beware the Add-On Service

I always advise authors to be skeptical of add-on services — marketing especially. It's generally agreed in the industry that unless you've got very deep pockets, you just cannot hire it out to someone else, and that's even if the book is great. I've remarked many times that authors are as much, or more at fault, as the seller, for paying more than they need for services they do need, and for paying for services they don't need at all. Especially vulnerable are new authors, and authors recently dumped by their publishing companies – as they would like to believe it can be easy to simply throw money at a service to solve their problem, mewing in an almost deliberate naiveté, "I just want to write."

Lest I sound too harsh, I have often found the language on some of ASI's pages to be convincing, easily frightening uneducated authors into paying for a service that can be cheaply and easily done themselves.

When I voiced skepticism about their $699 book returns program (and $300 per year thereafter), since so few books — especially by self-publishers — are sold in brick-and-mortar bookstores anyway, ASI's senior vice president of marketing, Keith Ogoreck, responded, "I would disagree with you for sure on the booksellers return. No bookstores are going to order your book if it's not returnable. So we protect the bookstore and we protect the author. The interesting thing about our returnability, you are paid the royalty on those books, you don't have a chargeback on your returns in the royalties."

Sure, this would a great program if you are a very successful author, but it's a fact that the vast majority of self-publishers sell fewer than 200 books, and since bookstores are less and less effective places to sell books, it doesn't warrant it.

It was the language on Booktango's U.S. Copyright Registration service, along with the $150 price tag, that led to me write a post on how to easily and cheaply register your copyright electronically for $35 in 35 minutes.

The deal-breaker for me though, is that BookTango, and all of ASI's other publishing services, do not let you apply your own ISBNs to your books. This makes the book exclusive, which means that you can't switch services without the hassle of retiring and republishing your book elsewhere. Here's the story of how one author overcame the ISBN trap.

Beware the ISBN Trap

Larry Jaffee wants his book back. "Albert Square & Me: The Actors of EastEnders" is based on 18 years of interviews with actors from the popular BBC show. He chose iUniverse to publish his book because "I was looking for a one-stop shop that would run the interference I needed." He bought their Premier program for $899 (on special from $1099), which included the ISBN and bar code acquisition, and distribution   in   the U.K. Getting into U.K. wholesalers Bertrams and Gardners was an integral part of his marketing plan, as the 25th anniversary of the show was coming up.

"They even talked me into an additional $699 for a program to handle bookstore returns," he said.

The only problem?

"The U.K. bookstores didn't order it because it was a [print-on-demand] book."

Two years later, in 2012, Jaffee let me know that "I successfully extricated myself from iUniverse, republished Albert Square & Me and a new one (Walford State of Mind) by going direct to Lightning Source." He told me "it's great earning about $8 per book from an Amazon sale instead of the less than $2 garnered from iUniverse. Live and learn."

Jaffee, a man with a deep connection to and passion for his topic, bumped up his publishing strategy and, instead of just focusing on the British TV show EastEnders, broadened his vision to publish a new, advertising-based magazine, UK:Cue – British Film, Theatre & Television On Both Sides of the Atlantic.

Jaffee's marketing plan included printing 2,000 copies of a prototype magazine "to prove the concept to investors and major advertisers." The magazine debuted at the Olivier Awards satellite link from London to New York's Lincoln Center, and was distributed later at "BritWeek," a celebration of British culture in California. Jaffee also started blogging for Huffington Post UK, raised $5,000 through a Kickstarter campaign to get the funds required to print the prototype, and "recruited a terrific Anglo-American editorial team of professionals."

Jaffee's mistake is a common one — most writers do not understand the importance of buying their own ISBN numbers, and for convenience, allow it to be bought and controlled by a third-party (Author Solutions/iUniverse) instead of owning it themselves, which effectively traps the book with that company.

Don't get me wrong, many reputable companies will assign your book one of their ISBN numbers for you, for free, but most of them agree you should buy your own, and provide the service only because authors are so reluctant to do it themselves, fearing unnecessarily that it is difficult and expensive. Sure, it's a couple hundred dollars more than free, but that's a small price to pay to make your book portable among vendors. See the chapter on buying ISBNs in this book for step-by-step instructions.

Great Distribution, Paltry Profits

It's important to realize author services companies do not make their money from selling books — they make money from convincing authors to buy their services. An author services company sells your book through their program to online resellers like Amazon and in their own online store, and they allow you to buy an inventory of your own book for a set price.

For example, when Jaffee sold "EastEnders" on Amazon, he got about $2 per book after iUniverse took their cut. By buying his own ISBN and printing with Lightning Source, he quadrupled his profits. (It's worth noting that Amazon's CreateSpace offers similar pricing, and is easier for self-publishing newbies to use than Lightning Source, which is really a publisher-services company.)

Since brick-and-mortar bookstores don't buy books unless they can be returned without cost, some author services companies seduce self-publishers with "returnability" programs. (The cost for ASI's Author House program is $749.00) Don't be. It's difficult for established publishing companies to get most of their authors stocked in stores, and a returns program won't help much for an unknown.

Print On Demand: The Proof is in the Price

When author Serena Bartlett published her first GrassRoutes travel guidebook with the self-publishing platform Lulu back in 2009, she was delighted with the ease of the process but said "the print quality was awful. Pages fell out, bindings cracked, covers curled." Just a couple of years later, print-on-demand technology and machinery had improved so much that it's difficult to tell an on-demand or short-run book from a traditionally printed book from an offset printer.

Lisa Alpine, a member of my Wild Writing Women group, is a book-birthing coach and author of "Exotic Life: Laughing Rivers, Dancing Drums and Tangled Hearts."Printed proofs can cost up to $45 from Lightning Source and other traditional printing companies, but I upload my latest PDF privately to CreateSpace, and order a copy delivered in the mail for under $10," she said. "It's an affordable way to see how the book will look before I send it out into the world, to play with the design, fonts, line spacing and margins, and even to proofread it in it's final form."

Your Book, Your Team

More and more people with serious ambitions for their book are realizing that author services companies aren't necessarily the place to go. More people are starting their own businesses and professionally producing their own books.

In terms of working with consultants, remember that paid professionals like editors and designers are as proud of their work as you are of your own, and they're a joy to collaborate with. For book authors this is, luckily, the more rewarding choice.

Whether you're looking for fast, easy, and cheap, or a sophisticated enhanced e-book solution, the answers lie in the chapters ahead. Especially important is to own your book and your book data. This requires that you buy your own ISBNs from Bowker, as described in the next chapter.

3

Buying ISBNs and Getting into the 'Books in Print' Database

Do not make the mistake of allowing a third party to assign one of their ISBNs to your book instead of using one that you bought directly from Bowker. Whoever is the "publisher of record" controls the book data, which is how retailers and readers find your book. If it's not you, your book is essentially trapped with that vendor's publishing service.

To rectify the problem of a vendor-assigned ISBN isn't simple. It is a long and tedious process of retiring, or discontinuing the ISBN — your book title — at which point your potential customers will only see that it is no longer available. Then you'll need to re-publish it with your own ISBN.

If you had bought your own ISBN, you could have simply stopped using the service and distributed your print or e-book with whichever vendor you choose.

If you want to take your book out of print, or discontinue it and point to a new edition, all you have to do is log into the MyIdentifiers website and make the changes so that customers magically see the new edition without any confusion whatsoever.

This is a favor the company you're abandoning will rarely be willing to do. And be aware that some subsidy and vanity presses do not even give you the option of applying your own ISBN. That's a warning sign. Don't hire them.

Betcha Can't Buy Just One

Buy 10 ISBN numbers, not just one. Why? Because you need one ISBN for the print version of your book, and a separate ISBN for each e-book sales channel. It's important to understand which channels and formats need different ISBNs. Here's an explanation.

The ISO 2108:2005 standard was developed for traditional publishing, not for self-publishers. So, unlike self-publishers, traditional publishing assigns a different ISBN for the print version of a book and each e-book format: mobi, EPUB, PDF, etc.

But self-publishers usually fit into one of two categories: those who have e-book files in-hand, and those who use a service to format and distribute their e-book.

If you have e-book files in-hand (EPUB, PDF, mobi/KF8), and you want to upload them one-by-one to e-book retailers like Barnes & Noble, Amazon, Apple, etc., then the traditional publishing standard applies to you. That is, assign one ISBN to your print edition, one to the PDF version, one to EPUB, one to KF8/mobi and so on.

However, most self-publishers find it more efficient to sell through services like Aerbook Maker, CreateSpace, BookBaby, Smashwords, KDP and Vook. If this is you, create separate book files with separate ISBNs to send to each of these vendors/sales channels. For example, you'll need one ISBN for the CreateSpace print edition, one ISBN for the e-book distributed by Smashwords, one ISBN for the e-book you upload to Amazon KDP, and one ISBN for the multimedia book distributed by Vook or Aerbook.

So even though Smashwords sells PDF, EPUB, mobi and many other formats, it's only necessary to supply one ISBN for the Smashwords version.

Your print version is considered a single format, no matter where you sell it. So assign a single ISBN to your print version though you may print and distribute it using CreateSpace or another service, or by hand from a bulk printing by one or more short-run or offset printing company.

Buy Your ISBNs and Bar Codes

1. Visit www.myidentifiers.com and create an account.
2. Buy a block of 10 ISBN numbers. (You will need to assign a different ISBN to each form of your book: print book, audio book and separately available e-books.)

3. When your book is ready to publish, find the ISBN number in your list, and fill out all the metadata in the Bowker system so that your book will be discoverable to readers and distributors.

4. If you plan to publish more than one book, think about purchasing a SAN (Standard Address Number), a publisher identifier. The use of the SAN significantly reduces billing errors, books shipped to the wrong points, and errors in payments and returns.

5. Buy a bar code for the book(s) you are printing but only once you have decided on the retail price of your book. (You cannot change it once it's assigned.) An e-book does not need a bar code unless you have designed it to be downloaded and printed, and scanned by a bar code reader.

Add Your Title to the Books In Print Database

Once you've published your book, add your title to the Books In Print database. This database is managed by Bowker, the service who supplies libraries, booksellers, publishers and other information professionals with the details you provided about your book.

1. Go to www.bowkerlink.com, create an account and log in.

2. Enter the ISBN number of the first book you wish to register.

3. Click on the red arrow to display the book information.

4. Fill in the information required, using carefully-chosen metadata.

Replacing or retiring an ISBN

If you want to take a book out of circulation, change the "Title Status" from "Active" using the drop-down menu.

If you publish a new edition of a book, log in to your Bowker account and display the ISBN data for the old edition. Select, "Replaced by ISBN" and enter the ISBN number of the new edition.

What Next?

Now that you own your book data, you can create your book in any format, and use any service to publish it in print and e-book formats, as well as a book app.

4

The Easiest, Cheapest, Fastest Way to Self-Publish Your Book

You are excited to self-publish, but sorting through the sheer quantity of offerings, claims and technologies is overwhelming. You can spend weeks and even months researching solutions, but here's the quick answer: Use a combination of Smashwords and Kindle Direct Publishing for your e-book, and CreateSpace for your print-on-demand book.

Publish Your E-Book

Using a combination of two services, Smashwords and Amazon Kindle Direct Publishing (KDP), is one of the easiest, cheapest and fastest ways to get your e-book in stores for the most complete distribution to online stores. With this combination, your book gets:

- converted into all the major e-book and app formats
- the widest possible distribution to online retailers
- the ability to be read on all the important devices
- a non-exclusive contract
- no up-front fees
- and 50-85% percent of net sales

Create Your Smashwords E-Book

Smashwords is a technology company founded in 2009 by Mark Coker in response to his frustration with publishing his own book. The company pioneered e-book creation technology and remains at the forefront of the industry. Authors have a love/hate relationship with the Smashwords e-book conversion tool, charmingly called "the meatgrinder." But when your Word document is formatted properly, the meatgrinder converts your book to many different formats for distribution to the markets you choose.

Smashwords' commission is 15% or less of net sales, which works out to slightly under 10% of the retail price when your book sells at their retailers. For example, a $10.00 e-book sold at one of their retail partners (Apple, B&N, etc.) earns you $6.00 and earns Smashwords $1.00. The same book sold at Smashwords earns you about $8.00. Here's how to create an e-book with Smashwords:

1. Create an account with Smashwords
2. Format your e-book in a Microsoft Word doc file in compliance with the Smashwords Style Guide (templates are available), or hire someone to do it for you. (See the company's FAQ to get a list of formatters and book cover designers if you need them.)
3. Assign a unique ISBN to the Smashwords version of your e-book. (Instructions for buying ISBNs from Bowker, including why you should not let anyone else buy them for you are explained in another chapter of this book.)
4. Follow the instructions to upload the interior and cover, and include carefully chosen keywords, as described in the chapter on metadata.
5. Join the Smashwords Premium Catalog and agree to all the contracts.
6. Submit the document and check the boxes next to the formats you want the Smashwords "meatgrinder" to generate.

If you have a perfectly-formatted EPUB file already, Smashwords Direct is a new publishing option that lets you upload it. The service bypasses their meatgrinder conversion engine so that your more highly formatted e-book can take advantage of the vast Smashwords distribution network.

Create Your Amazon Kindle E-Book

Though Smashwords creates a Kindle file for your readers to download, it does not distribute to the Amazon Kindle store (though a deal seems perpetually pending.) But the good news is that the .doc file you created for Smashwords is similar to their formatting requirements, so you can upload a Kindle version to the Amazon store yourself. Here's how:

1. Make a copy of the Smashwords doc file and rename it.
2. Assign a different ISBN to the KDP version of your e-book.
3. Make changes as required to comply with KDP formatting guidelines.
4. Create a KDP account.
5. Follow the instructions to upload the interior, cover, and provide keywords so that readers can find your book.

Check out this video that provides authors and publishers an overview on publishing a digital book to the Amazon Kindle Store: http://bit.ly/14poljA.

Alternately, if you're creating a print-on-demand book first, do it with CreateSpace and pay them $65 to convert it to KDP format for you.

Amazon has an exclusive marketing program called Kindle Select, that can give your book a marketing boost. But if you do this, you can not publish or distribute it anywhere else for a number of weeks. Some authors find it is worth it.

Microsoft Word Styles

The key to using these two services successfully is to start with a properly formatted Microsoft Word document, as defined in the Smashwords Style Guide. If you are proficient in Word, you know how to use heading and paragraph styles, but if you don't, it's not that difficult. (Lynda.com has a great tutorial and a free trial.)

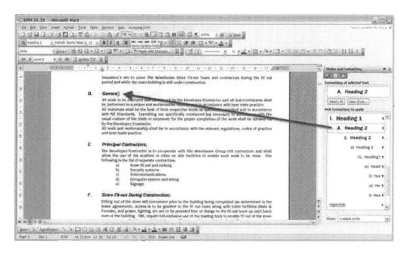

If you don't have the time, patience or ability to implement styles, don't worry, Smashwords has a list of people who will format your book and design your book cover, for astoundingly reasonable fees.

Create Your Print-on-Demand (POD) Book

CreateSpace is an author services company owned by Amazon and is therefore a direct channel to getting into the biggest bookstore in the world. Use one of their Microsoft Word templates to format your book, and the Photoshop PDF file for your book cover. Or if your book has already been professionally designed and formatted, you can simply upload the PDF files.

Sign up for the CreateSpace Expanded Distribution Channel (EDC) for $25, which makes your print book visible to both brick-and-mortar and online book resellers, just like any book sold by a major publisher.

Buy Your Own ISBNs and Create Your Metadata

You'll need to assign a separate ISBN to each edition of your book, so buy a pack of 10 for $250 from the ISBN Agency run by Bowker. It is very, very important to do this yourself and not let any service provide you with an ISBN. You need to be able to log into Bowker with your own credentials in order to create and update the data that is disseminated about your book to all the various markets. So far you'll need three ISBNs, two for the Smashwords and Amazon KDP sales channels, and one for the CreateSpace print version. Find out more about ISBNs and metadata in a later chapter of this book.

What Does All This Cost?

When all is said and done, you've got an e-book and a print book for around $500. Let's break it down:

- $45-$125 for formatting
- $100-$200 for a cover design
- $250 for a block of 10 ISBN numbers from Bowker
- $25 for the CreateSpace Expanded Distribution Channel

This is my best solution for the cheapest and easiest way to create and distribute your e-book and print book. But if you really believe in your book, have done the market research, and are serious about becoming a bona-fide independent publisher committed to reaching the mass market, you're going to need to spend a lot more time and money on editing, designing, marketing and promotion, beyond just the fast, cheap, easy solution I've outlined above.

What's the Cost of Real Success?

I estimate that the budget required to create a quality self-published trade paperback book *that competes in the general marketplace* is a bare minimum of $5,000. Here's a list of some items needed to put your book respectably alongside those from traditional publishers, with minimum price tags. The lower the price, the more you have to do yourself, so bump it up if you want to be completely hands-off:

- $1,000 Professional editing (developmental, line editing, proofreading)
- $1,000 Professional cover design
- $1,000 Marketing and promotion
- $500 Advance Reading Copies (ARCs) and postage
- $500 Website design and creation, not including domain name purchases, PayPal shopping cart, mailing list management, and related site costs
- $500 Photography, logo design, and other branding items

- $65 Membership in one or two professional publishers associations like SPAN

My "Self-Publishing Boot Camp Guide for Authors" (http://selfpubbootcamp.com/) has a page full of budget items and activities that detail each step.

It's Okay to Just Test the Waters

There's nothing wrong with test-driving your book using the fast, cheap, and easy method sketched out here before committing to investing thousands more. You can use CreateSpace to print many versions of your book, ordering one at a time to evaluate the design and format, to edit and proofread — before making it available for public consumption. That's what POD is all about, after all — printing on demand — and it can be an exciting and satisfying journey. Just make sure to buy your own ISBN number from Bowker, so that when you become more familiar with the publishing process, you are not locked in to using any one vendor, and can move your book production and distribution to any vendor or combination of vendors you like.

Need More Formatting?

So this was the easy, cheap and fast way to publish your book, and you don't really have to understand much about book formatting to do it. In the next chapter, let's delve into the details of the different formats for the different reading devices.

5

Formats: Print, E-Books, Rich Media Books, Apps and Games

The previous chapter demonstrated the easy, cheap and fast way to publish a simple book in print and all the e-book formats for delivery to an array of e-reading devices. This chapter dives deeper into the different formats, from PDF for a print book, to a simple e-book for the Kindle and EPUB devices, or a multimedia extravaganza for delivery on the new tablets. And the next chapter will help you choose the right tool for the transmedia book or app you envision. For now, let's get familiar with formats.

E-Book and Print Formats

The major print book and e-book formats to be especially aware of are PDF, EPUB, Fixed-Layout EPUB, Mobi and Kindle Format 8. There are many more, some legacy, some experimental, but these are the formats that will get you to most readers.

Adobe PDF – Portable Document Format

Most of us have used the free Adobe Reader to read PDF documents online. Maybe you have created PDFs by "printing" to PDF from Microsoft Word, or "exporting" to PDF from InDesign. When you convert documents, forms, graphics and web pages to PDF, they look just like they would if printed. Anyone can read a PDF document using the free Adobe Reader software or the mobile app. If you're creating a print book — whether traditionally "offset" printed, printed with a short-run service, or printing on-demand with a service like CreateSpace — you'll need to provide them with a PDF document.

Many people still read books on their computer screens, so it's good to offer a PDF for download along with all the various e-book formats.

EPUB and Fixed-Layout EPUB

Unlike PDF formatted documents, content in EPUB format reflows, shrinking and expanding to fit the screen of any size device. Readers can change the font size and colors, search text and enjoy multimedia, such as ambient music and narration that's directly embedded in the file or linked out to the Internet. EPUB is the most popular e-book format and you definitely need to provide it for the iPad, Nook, Kobo and Sony readers. All the tools and services recommended in this book create EPUB formats except Amazon's Kindle Direct Publishing system, which only publishes for the Kindle format, described below.

Content delivered in fixed-format EPUB is different in that the content is fixed, like a PDF document, but it's like an e-book in that you can search for text and enjoy links and multimedia. But readers cannot change how the book flows inside their device. You, the book designer, determine what fonts are used, and you can make text wrap around graphics, preserving the aspect ratio of a page, with page breaks occurring where you want them to.

This all sounds lovely until you consider that many users will be frustrated that they can't enlarge the font or see a sentence in its entirety without zooming in and out and panning back and forth. So ask yourself if your audience will read your book on an iPhone or a tablet. Is the book better in fixed layout? Will readers expect the book to be a controlled experience, or will they want to reflow the text to suit their device? Heavily illustrated cookbooks, children's books and art catalogs make good fixed-format EPUB books. Novels? No.

You can use iBooks Author to create fixed-layout e-books for the iPad, but Aerbook Maker is your best bet if you want to get into iBooks, plus Kobo, Kindle KF8, ePub 3 and in HTML5 for the web. They also create fixed-layout books for the Nook. BookBaby can create fixed-layout EPUB for Apple.

Mobi and Kindle Format 8 (KF8)

Kindle Format 8 replaced the Mobi format that the old Kindle readers use. If you're doing it yourself using a tool like Scrivener, PressBooks,   or Folium   Book   Studio,   then download KindleGen 2 to generate Kindle Format 8 (KF8) content from a EPUB, or even HTM and, XHTML. Once you convert the Kindle File, download Kindle Previewer so you can see how your book will look on Kindle devices and apps. Again, Aerbook Maker, BookBaby and Vook can create e-books in this format.

Enhanced E-Books

Just because you can create an enhanced e-book doesn't mean you should. "If it's a book about music history, having music people can play at certain points in the book can be useful," said Amazon's Jeff Bezos, in an interview with USA Today. "You're not going to make Hemingway better by adding animations."

"Enhancements should only be in support of the central proposition of the writing rather than a 'I can do it therefore I will do it' approach," said Peter Collingridge of UK-based Enhanced Editions. New Media storyteller J.C. Hutchins also has some good advice, such as avoiding "self-congratulatory 'behind the scenes' content such as author bios, old drafts of your manuscripts."

A few years ago I produced a multimedia e-zine, Ireland: The Sacred and the Profane, using InDesign. It was highly formatted, and included a lot of graphics, photos, type treatments, audio and video files. I offered it as a free download directly from the Wild Writing Women website until I found it easier to offer it via the document sharing site Scribd. The magazine was very time-consuming to produce, but incredibly rewarding and the enhancements offered readers a lot of extra value. InDesign remains a great tool for this kind of work.

But early on, the iPad's capabilities made it the enhanced e-book platform of choice. The "amplified edition" of Ken Follette's Pillars of the Earth has a huge cache of multimedia, an interactive character tree, video and still images from the Starz television series, the author's multimedia diary with his impressions of bringing the book to the screen, interviews with the actors, director and producers and music from the series. Today, Aerbook Maker produces the same kind of content for all devices, not just the iPad, so it's difficult to recommend iBooks Author or any other proprietary system unless you are specifically targeting iPad readers.

How much does creating an enhanced e-book or app cost in terms of time and money? It took me months to create the Ireland magazine in InDesign, and would have cost over $10,000 if I hadn't been working for free. So when Collingridge quoted $8,000 to $15,000 for enhanced e-book production, that sounded about right. Today, Mimetic Books quotes prices from $850 to $2500. But today's tools have made the process so easy that just about anyone can put together an enhanced e-book for about $300, plus your time, of course.

Another example is Sutro Media, targeted to travel guidebook authors. Sutro Media created a browser-based tool to let publishers upload material to a content management system, which then gets ported into Objective C on the back end. Co-founder Kevin Collins says, "These apps do things that books can't possibly do. For example, you can use all the photos you had to leave out in their book versions, and include live maps and hyperlinks, too."

Sutro does not require the author pay any up-front costs, but they carefully evaluate proposed projects. Their payment model is a revenue-sharing agreement with a royalty split of 30% each going to Sutro, Apple, and the author, with the remaining 10% going to their in-house editor.

How About a Book-Based App or Game?

When you've got so much material that linear is no longer practical, then it might be time to consider an app as an add-on product to your book.

"Book-based apps are more likely to be ancillary products with complex graphics and page layouts that can't be handled in something that auto-flows," says Michel Kripalani, founder of Oceanhouse Media. "That's where you cross the line into the need for custom code." Kripalani assembled a team of former interactive CD-ROM and game developers to start his business, and has built over 100 apps since the company was founded in January 2009. But today you can build a book-based app using do-it-yourself tools.

"Children's books are especially ripe for apps, and compliment the e-book edition," noted Kripalani in an interview with Book Business Magazine. Oceanhouse has also created a variety of card decks, calendars and spoken word apps inspired by books from Hay House and Chronicle Books.

The price tag for a complex, quality book-based app? Until last year, it was "In the five-figures," said Kripalini, requiring a team that "includes C++/Objective C programmers, graphic designers, professional actors and custom narration, music soundtrack and sound effects, interactivity, editors and page layout designers for the different devices."

But Aerbook Maker and Kwik make the process easy and cheap — under $250 in many cases.

The next chapter dives deeper into enhanced e-books and apps, and provides guidance on the best tools for creating them.

6

Tools for Creating Sophisticated Enhanced E-Books and Apps

In the previous chapter you learned about e-book formats that create simple immersive reading experiences — such as a novel — and sophisticated, transmedia books, also called enhanced e-books.

What is an Enhanced E-Book?

In a nutshell, an e-book is a digital snapshot of a book. An enhanced e-book adds multimedia and interactive features that interrupts the linear story. And a book app is based on a book but acts more like a game with multiple pathways that require the user to interact instead of simply scrolling and clicking.

Enhanced e-books are also referred to as rich media books, book mashups, enriched, hybrid and amplified books. The media and interactivity is provided by you, the self-publisher, who collects and integrates music, audio, video and color photo slideshows, news feeds, illustrations and background materials. You may also provide searchable text, tilt scrolling, internal and external links and Flash animations into the linear story.

What's an App?

A book app can do everything an enhanced e-book does, but crosses the line from linear storytelling to non-linear storytelling, allowing the user to choose from multiple pathways and select from a potentially huge number of photos, videos, audio files, illustrations, hyperlinks and interactivity. A lot of the really sophisticated book apps you see are third-party software programs requiring a programmer with C++ or

Apple's Objective C programming skills. But increasingly, author tools like iBook Author and Aerbook Maker easily handle the job.

E-Books in App Stores

Much confusion arises from the fact that so many books are simply bundled as apps so they can be sold in an app store. There are more e-books than games in the iPhone App Store, even though there seems to be little point to e-book app-wrapping when compared with more elegant, library-based e-book stores and their e-reader apps (the iBookstore download to the iBook e-reader app, for example) — which gives customers a more consistent user experience and keeps the device desktop uncluttered. Still, people buy books from the app stores, so app wrapping happens.

The Tools

The development of user-friendly tools for authors to build rich-media books boomed in 2012 and are being finessed in 2013. Scrivener, Pressbooks, Vook and BookBaby, among others, are capable of including multimedia in your book. But to create beautiful, graphically-enriched enhanced e-books and apps, you'll want to use the tools described in this chapter.

Aerbook Maker is a browser-based, drag-and-drop tool that works much like presentation applications (like Keynote and PowerPoint). Kwik is a plug-in that extends Photoshop CS5 to create pages of a book and even animations. Mimetic Books is at work on a plug-in to Adobe InDesign.

Aerbook Maker

If you're writing an illustrated children's' book, a book of photography, art, or any other heavily graphic book, Aerbook Maker is for you. It's easy to drag and drop your files into a window in the web browser. You can drop in photos, audio, video, text boxes, scene animation and interactivity, then rearrange them and apply styles, colors and frames.

When you're done, export your content to all the major e-book formats — or to HTML5 for viewing on the web — and soon you'll be able to print.

A built-in social media feature lets readers share any page of your book on Twitter, Facebook and other networks. Like Kwik and many other tools for authors, Aerbook is evolving. Though books are not fully or officially supported until iOS 6, your book will probably already work on the iPad today.

The tool is cloud-based, so whether you're just one author, or partnering with a designer or an entire team, the project is scalable and centrally available.

Aerbook Maker's pricing structure is based on export credits at $29 each or $99 for five exports. This removes the Aerbook watermark and generates a final version to download directly to devices and place with e-book retailers. Their services include book and app distribution, and they will help you build your book for a reasonable fee.

The Kwik Photoshop Plugin

Kwik is now in release 2.0 with a portfolio of cross-platform e-books that include "Fire Cupid" (featured in the Wall Street Journal, TIME, the Washington Times and others), Frederick "Spin" (which soared to the No. 2 e-book in the Dutch App Store), and "Sparky the Shark" (a beloved, award-winning children's tale).

Kwik's capabilities allow much more than creation of a simple color book. You can add audio, sound effects, buttons, timers, actions, drag and drop objects, linear animation, sprite sheets, movie clips, even path animation. Children's book authors will be interested in the ability to sync audio to text so that the words are highlighted during playback. If you have items for sale in the iTunes App Store or Google Play, you can insert in-app purchases. Output your book to a universal app or iPad, iPhone, Kindle Fire, Nook Color or other Android device.

Kwik's creator, Alex Souza, holds a master's degree in Digital Design. In 1995, he was the first developer of a Shockwave game in his native Brazil, and in 2000 was a runner-up for the iBest Top 3 award, Brazil's most important Internet award. Later he worked for IBM and Microsoft, creating applications and marketing Microsoft Office, Expression and Silverlight.

"There are too many updates to 2.0 to list, but physics is a major thing in the new version," said Souza, "so the game-making capabilities have improved." Kwik 2 costs $249.99 for a new license and $149.99 for an upgrade. The free trial version will allow you to export up to four project pages.

Mimetic Books

Photojournalist David Gross of Mimetic Books put together the App of the Week winner "A Wild Flight of the Imagination: The Story of the Golden Gate Bridge," for its 75th anniversary. The free e-book weaves interactive photographs, artwork, letters and newspaper clippings together with music, audio recordings and video.

Gross is a photographer who can code, and he invented his own way of importing his projects directly from Adobe InDesign (the tool that book designers use) and exporting the results to XML. Gross says that Mimetic Books plans to offer an InDesign plug-in so that photographers and artists can create books to publish to the iPad and Nook. In the meantime, they do it for you. You choose from a number of designs, then send Mimetic the picture files. They can create a chapter from a properly captioned collection of photos in Lightroom or from captioned JPEG pictures. Or you can hire them to do full-service graphic design, photo-editing, copywriting, editing, animation and custom programming.

Gross said that as well as using InDesign, "I am working on ways of using Google Apps, WordPress and a custom browser-based editor to create books. As well, I am investigating whether Kwik can create plug-ins for books — Kwik excels in making complex animations, so why should I?"

Regarding pricing, Gross said that "I was offering book apps starting at $850, but I found that clients did not have enough experience in graphic design to deliver 100% complete materials. The extra work I have to do to prepare clients' pictures, sound, and video, and the multiple changes clients make during the creation of the book, I have found a book project generally costs between $5,000 and $15,000. In addition, custom 'interactive' pages also raise the price. But, I can produce a basic book app relatively cheaply using my system."

So What's an E-Book and What's an App?

Yes. The lines are blurring as content becomes portable among a variety of devices.

"Book apps are different from e-books," Gross explained. "E-books are data files which are displayed with readers. EPUB is one of the best-known data file formats designed for books of text (not fixed-format). A 'book app' is an app — a stand-alone program — that is a book. It's a weird idea, actually, a temporary effect of the state of publishing software and the market. In a rational world, it wouldn't exist, and I don't expect such things to exist in few years. Instead, we will have a few e-book file formats that the different devices can read and display."

The Corona SDK

If you're geeky enough to know that SDK stands for Software Development Kit, you might be interested in the reasons these e-book and app platform developers chose the Corona SDK to power Aerbook Maker and Kwik export-to-app capabilities. David Rangel, COO of Corona Labs, says that "Corona integrates a number of advanced technologies such as OpenGL (widely adopted 2D and 3D graphics API), Box2D (a 2D physics engine for games), physics and more, to allow developers to create great mobile content. If e-book platforms wanted to replicate these features on their own, it would take them loads of development time and expertise. By building to Corona SDK, they save a great deal of time and get to take advantage of our platform's offerings."

Adding to the previous point, Rangel said, "Corona allows developers to build apps for both iOS and Android, from a single code base. If e-book platforms want to support both of these operating systems, they would need to spend a lot of time and energy building in that support. As we add in more features and platform support for CoronaSDK, Kwik and Aerbook Maker automatically reap the benefits."

Designers and illustrators are attracted to the SDK's core engine because of its popularity in the mobile space. Kwik and Aerbook Maker provide the added advantage of allowing e-book authors to create impressive content without the need for code.

7

The Need for Professional Editing and Design

Many self-publishers create niche books that sell to a captive audience that needs the information, but some of us write books that need to compete in the general marketplace. If you want to compete with the books that big-publishing puts in the stores, you'll need to spend the money for professional editing and design for both the cover and interior book files.

About Standard Templates

The book interior and cover design tools that printing and author services companies provide are very easy to use, but many are also proprietary. This means that you have to start all over again if you want to move your book to another company. It's also worth noting that both editing and design should really be outsourced to professionals. Nobody can can do it all.

"It's a crapshoot," said Joel Friedlander, a professional book designer who has spent time correcting bad book covers and interior designs that suffer from poor font choices, inadequate margins and poorly thought out images. "I have a book from CreateSpace on my desk with the odd page numbers on the left, the even ones on the right, set completely in Times and Times Bold. What a disaster! These companies sell a paint-by-the-numbers standard template that may be completely inappropriate for your book's intended market. It brands the author as an amateur, or worse, incompetent. Find a designer who will respect your work, treat you as an individual, and give you a book that you can proudly sell against the best books on the shelf."

This is not to say that CreateSpace — or, in fact, any print vendor — is at fault. They provide a great set of print-on-demand tools and services that work with their printing process. But they'll just as happily print a badly-designed book as a good one.

Take a look at Friedlander's series of articles about book design (http://www.thebookdesigner.com/articles/) to get an idea of the complexity of design. Find an editor by asking around at local writing and publishing organizations, and by asking online groups. Get recommendations and clarity on pricing, and start with one chapter to make sure you're compatible. Print proofs and commit to perfection.

Finding a Good Editor

Lisa Alpine's search for a copy editor turned up many who replied to her carefully spelled-out requirements with a cursory email stating, "I'd love to take a look at your book!" and no details on pricing or process. Alpine says the editor she hired was "the only candidate who professionally returned a price sheet with clear descriptions of the various levels of editing with prices clearly stated for services from proofreading to conceptual [developmental] editing."

She hired her to edit one chapter to see if their personalities fit.

"The working relationship between editor and author is so close," said Alpine,"that it's essential you're on the same page, so to speak." This is also true for working with designers. Alpine hired Lyn Bishop to consult with her on the cover for her anthology Exotic Life, though she also did part of the work herself since she's somewhat proficient using Photoshop.

In terms of working with consultants, remember that paid professionals are as proud of their work as you are of your own, and they can be a joy to collaborate with. For book authors this is, luckily, the more rewarding choice.

"I really savor each step in the process, and getting involved so I don't have to be stressed out and mystified," said Alpine. "You know, we used to throw manuscripts to a publisher and hope for the best. I think it's a real privilege to be able to have control of your own book."

About Editors

During the book development phase, you may want to hire a **Developmental Editor** to help you shape your book. This kind of editor is familiar with the books in your market, and can assist with the big picture structure like narrative arc, plot and theme. A great book for understanding these elements is "Wired for Story: The Writer's Guide to Using Brain Science to Hook Readers from the Very First Sentence" (http://amzn.to/VQggBQ). If you're lucky enough to be a member of a writing group, it may play the part of a Developmental Editor for you, letting you know (gently!) that Chapter 1 should be thrown out, or that guy you introduced in Chapter 5 never appeared again so, since his presence doesn't further the plot or develop a theme, get rid of him!

A **Copy Editor** is what people think of most of the time when they think of "Editor." Copy editors concentrate on the written text, the style and accuracy, grammar, spelling and punctuation.

A **Proofreader** is the last editor you'll need in the editorial cycle. Yes, get your family, friends and colleagues to catch those pesky typos, but hire a professional for the very last round. Someone who has never seen the book before.

About Designers

There are two kinds of book designers, and they often have very different skills and talents.

Cover designers have the exciting artsy job of creating an eye-popping cover that competes, but still fits in to, the genre of book you have written. Smashwords has a good list of cover designers for e-books. Increasingly, people are finding designers and illustrators in places like Tumblr and in crowdsourcing sites like Design 99. Cover design has changed in the last years with the increased sales of books over the web, where covers are displayed in postage-stamp proportions.

Interior designers, on the other hand, are font geeks. They know about typography and ligature, kerning and gutters. They've been using Quark or InDesign for years. Interior designers are expert in the subtleties of the readers eye, and know how to make them comfortable, without any unexpected elements that interrupt the immersive reading process. They know where readers expect headers and footers, titles, and page numbers. Professional interior designers are essential for your print book but, excepting fixed-layout EPUB and KF8 e-book formatting, they're not necessary for designing an e-book, since the reader sets the font.

Now, on to Doing Business as a Publisher

In this section of this book we focused on authoring and book creation. The following section focuses on doing business as a publisher, which includes marketing, outsourcing things like editing and design, copyrighting your work and selling.

PART II

Going Above and Beyond

8

Metadata: The Essential Passive Marketing Tool

The easiest book marketing you can do is passive marketing with metadata — that is, to attach words to your book that the search engines can find, so that the online retailers and bookstores can find you, and so your readers, reviewers, bloggers and journalists can find you.

Metadata is a core component of digital information and news; so good book metadata is good book marketing. It's also an essential tool for all self-publishers. Think of metadata as your strongest marketing partner. When you list your book in the right places with the right words, search engines can more easily find you, which means that readers can more easily find you.

Metadata is simply data about data, words about words. In the semantically driven matrix of search, all words have a value, and "key" words have more value still. These keywords must be strategically selected and then placed where they can do the most good. Creating metadata tags for your work is a marketing challenge that requires both editing skill and narrative common sense.

The word is unfamiliar and sounds a little daunting, but it's simple. If you know who your audience is and you can fill out a form, you can create metadata for your book. Here's what you need to know about providing metadata for your book record on the Bowker system, where you bought your ISBN numbers, and for all your web activities.

Identify Your Keywords

First, we must spill into search engine optimization (SEO) territory. The typical self-published author doesn't need to hire an SEO expert. Here are the steps to identifying a solid keyword list:

1. Imagine the words and short phrases your readers might enter into a search engine to find you and your book. Begin to eliminate the less important and more generic words and phrases from your list. Try to keep the number of repeated keywords to a maximum of three. The final list should be no more than 10 to 20 words with a 900 character maximum. This constitutes your "keywords" metadata and can be used for your book metadata, for creating tags on blog posts, and in your social media activities. Most major search engines (like Google) no longer factor in the keyword metatags at all in search results, so this just makes having effective TITLE and DESCRIPTION tags all the more important. (Similarly, your file names should be descriptive.)

2. Once you have your keyword list, edit the TITLE metatag of your web pages to describe each page in a nutshell. Make it informative to users first and search engines second. Set a maximum of 60 characters, including spaces, and be sure to feature your top keywords.

3. Finally, considering both your keywords and your TITLE, draft a succinct but keyword-rich DESCRIPTION of your book. Make this one informative to search engines first and users second. Keep it to a maximum of 150 characters.

Many website creation software and blog services provide you with simple forms where you can enter these various metatags, which it then inserts for you into the page's HTML "source" code which, under the covers, looks something like this:

```
<HTML>
<HEAD>
<META name="Title" content="Carla King: Motorcycle Adventure Traveler." />
<META name ="Description" content="Carla King authors books and
travelogues about her mostly solo motorcycle adventures in America, China,
India, Africa, and Europe." />
<META name="Keywords" content="carla king, motorcycle adventure, women
adventure travel writing, motorcycle touring, american borders, china
road, indian sunset, morocco, africa, europe, moto guzzi, harley-davidson,
kawasaki, suzuki, ural, royal enfield bullet" />
<\HEAD>
<\HTML>
```

Metadata also includes the "ALT" tags that offer short text descriptions for images. For example, the image of my book cover is tagged with: *ALT="American Borders: Read about a solo woman traveler exploring the USA on a Russian sidecar motorcycle."*

Also of great importance are the actual words on each web page and, more specifically, the words used in the opening paragraphs on the page, which need to indicate exactly what that page is about. So be sure to use "keyword-rich" sentences in those opening sections. Also, it is wise to begin each page of your website with words and not images.

Those are the basics, but people make entire careers of SEO. For a better understanding of metatagging, check out Wikipedia's entry: http://en.wikipedia.org/wiki/Metadata.

Metadata in Word Documents and Other Media

Believe it or not, search engines look inside documents and other media for clues about its content. Metadata resides in every Microsoft Word document you create, so that readers can find the author and company name (yours, or the owner of your bootlegged copy). To edit the data in a Word document, simply open the document and click File > Properties.

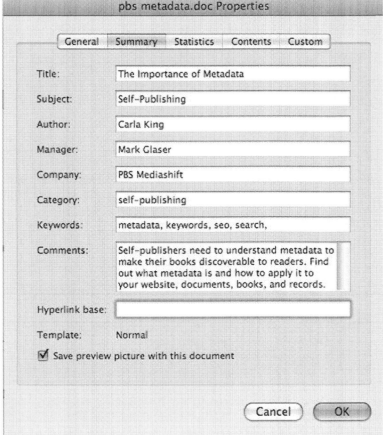

If you're publishing audio, video or any other media, make sure you edit the metadata inside the file you created using an application, too. For example, Audacity, a free, open-source program handy for recording music, podcasts and audiobooks, lets you insert ID3 tags that help identify the content to search engines and services like iTunes and Windows Media Player. Here's an example.

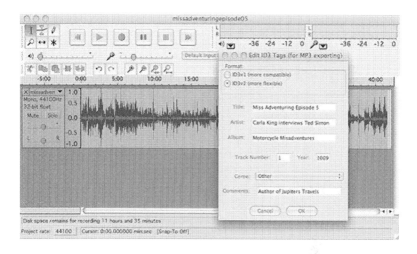

Metadata on Reseller Sites

E-book sites like Smashwords, social media publishing sites like Wattpad and Scribd, and e-tailers like Amazon and B&N, want their readers to discover and buy as many books as possible, which is why they make it easy for publishers to insert metadata. For example, if you've uploaded your book in Kindle format to Amazon, you will be prompted to insert the same kind of metadata as for the Bowker MyIdentifiers services site.

Metadata on Social Media Sites

Use all available information spaces on social media sites like Twitter, Facebook, LinkedIn and YouTube to get found and create incoming links to your book's web presence. Any keyword-rich author bio you can place anywhere on the web (including at the end of guest blogs and articles) is also valuable. An official Facebook author page (formerly a fan page, now a "like" page), gives you an opportunity to create more metadata that points to your book and also works nicely to create incoming links.

The Future of Metadata

As "new connections are formed and new data is added its value increases exponentially," wrote pundit Mike Cane in his post, "Dumb Ebooks Must Die Smart Ebooks Must Live" (http://bit.ly/10z9D5v).

With technical advances that allow us to sort through metadata inside books, readers may be able to search for "all fiction books set on Mars in any fictional year, published between 1940 and 1960," or even order up pieces of books, asking their device to "Show me all first paragraphs from fiction books published in May 2009."

"When you think about it, it seems remarkable that so much content does not have this sort of metadata already," wrote Martin Moore in an article for MediaShift, "How Metadata Can Eliminate the Need for Pay Walls" (http://to.pbs.org/19uyA7a). "It is like houses not having house numbers or zip codes. Or like movies not having opening or closing credits."

Metadata automates a formerly labor-intensive task by connecting readers to books more efficiently than ever before. The self-publisher who understands metadata levels the playing field to compete alongside big publishing — but only if you use it.

9

Social Media Marketing: Will Write for Publicity

Do you think that marketing your book is worth about an hour a day? After set-up, that's about all it takes to attend to the essentials: your blog, your email list, your Facebook Author Page, Amazon Central's Author Page, Twitter (and using Twitter hashtags), a professional presence on LinkedIn and, finally, one of the social publishing sites like Wattpad, Scribd, All Romance, or Red Room. There are certainly more places you can be, so if you like them, go forth and prosper. How much does it cost? Just your time and your words. Here are the social media marketing basics.

Social Media Rule of Thirds

The Social Media Rule of Thirds is this simple:

> 1. One third of the time, post information about you or your brand.
> 2. Another third of the time, post information or questions about your niche or area of interest. Comment, repost, retweet or reference others' work.
> 3. The final third of the time just be yourself, that whole person that your actual friends and family know and love. Post about your hobbies, opinions (maybe not political), and make sure to retweet, repost and link to things you find interesting as a person, even if it doesn't relate to your book or industry.

Asking questions gets results, too, often creating conversations on a topic you want to know more about. Being in an unfamiliar environment can get fun with Twitter. Say you're in San Francisco and you want to know where all the food carts are. Whip out your smartphone and check @sf-food-trucks and @streetfoodsf, then follow up with updates, including photos. On LinkedIn you might ask what the most important conferences are in your industry, with the aim of learning, speaking or selling books. Other examples of things you might post are links to news items, a discount for your book, a compliment to someone who has won an award or reached a goal, an event announcement, a sale on a product you believe in or an inspiring quote.

Pre-Book Beta Readers

If you haven't already published teasers from your book on a social publishing site (such as WattPad, All Romance, Red Room, Scribd) and created a Facebook author page, you should do that now, before you publish. It's a great way to start developing your platform, and your early readers can catch errors and give you input on your book before you go through all the time and expense of getting it formatted and distributed through more formal channels.

You can also start selling your text or PDF e-book directly from your own website or a store like Gumroad or Leanpub to your early readers, before you set up distribution of your final book to online retailers.

Facebook Author Page

Don't mix business with pleasure. Separate your personal Facebook page from your author persona, so your fans don't have to see irrelevant personal posts. Besides, "friends" max out at 5000 on Facebook, and you're going to have more fans than that, right? To create a Facebook Author Page you must first have a personal account with Facebook. Once you do, go to Create a Page and choose *Artist, Band* or *Public Figure*. Then choose *Author*. Some authors also like to create a *Book* page (under *Entertainment*) but the author page offers more flexibility as it allows you talk about other books you're writing and projects that relate to your book. So do yourself a favor and consolidate your efforts, keeping your fan base in one place. If you're a business author with a specific niche you may decide that a *Company* page suits you better than an *Author* page, because you can specify your industry niche. This can be useful especially if you also offer consulting services.

Once you set up your Facebook Author Page with images and some content, you're ready to go. Invite your Facebook friends to Like your page, put a Like button on your website, mention it in your blog, newsletter and Twitter account. Remember the social media rule of thirds and invite conversations by asking for critiques and reviews. You might even ask for suggestions or critiques of your upcoming book cover. Sharing updates on the progress of your as-yet-unfinished book can be fun and your immediate friends and family can spur a greater community interest. Offering excerpts and inviting feedback can be useful, too. Once your book is finished, you can create events, inviting your fans to a reading in a bookstore, coffee shop or a Google Hangout.

Amazon's Marketing Tools

Author Central (https://authorcentral.amazon.com/) is your author home page in the world's biggest bookstore. Along with your bio, you can can add multimedia, blog feeds, a Twitter feed and events. You can edit or correct Amazon's list of your books, claiming all your books so they're listed correctly on your bibliography. A *Sales* tab lets you track your book sales over time and check your current Amazon ranking. All your reviews are collected on one page. Amazon's other marketing tools for authors include KDP Select, an exclusive promotion program that you might decide can help you launch your book in a bigger way. Also check out Listmania, Shelfari, So you'd like to...guides, Amazon Associates, and Look Inside the Book.

Your Author Blog

It's astounding to many social media experts that many authors are so reluctant to blog. "But you're a writer!" they exclaim. And they're right. We do nanowritemo, freewriting and all kinds of writing exercises, but blogging? Yikes! That's self-promotion. Marketing. Scary! But authors are uniquely qualified to be blogging machines. So take advantage of your talents and share your words with the world, whether it's a daily tidbit, a weekly roundup, or a carefully-crafted post published monthly. It doesn't have to be market-y, just topical. It can even be a collection of other blog posts and news items you found interesting during that month.

WordPress is the most popular blogging platform, and tools like Pressbooks and Leanpub can actually consume your blog posts, just in case you ever want to create a book from them. Tumblr is a popular visual blogging tool popular with the Young Adult market. There are so many, it's difficult to recommend one for every author. Find out what your community is using and follow suit.

One note of caution. Install the blog tool in your own domain instead of using a free version. This makes your blog URL http://carlaking.com/blog and not http://wordpress.com/carlaking. This way you'll be able to change your blog tool at any time, exporting the current content and moving it to another platform, without losing readers. If you use a free service with the blog tool name in the URL, you'll lose your reader subscriptions when you change services.

Guest Blogging and Articles

Other bloggers, as well as magazine editors, are desperate for content. Not just any content, but carefully-crafted content on their topic. If you're a niche author, you probably already subscribe to related blog posts and magazines. Because you know the audience, you can offer an article or excerpt for free, in exchange for your author bio with a photo of your book cover and a Where to Buy link.

Querying busy bloggers and editors is often a waste of time. It's better to send them a copy of your e-book along with an article or post that is specifically designed for their audience. Do it well enough, and you may land a reprint, or even a regular column, in a place like Huffington Post or CNN.

Twitter

People either love it or hate it, but give Twitter some time to grow on you. Why? Because everybody's doing it, including a lot of journalists who hang out there trying to find sources. When you start to "get" hash tags, you'll find it an incredible publicity tool. (Always following the social media rule of thirds, of course.)

Use Twitter hashtags to categorize tweets by keyword. That way you can have a conversation, or get information, organized by topic. Clicking on a hashtagged word shows you all the tweets marked with that keyword. Sometimes they can become what's called a trending topic. #HurricaneSandy and #PussyRiot are examples of recent trends, with the world watching as the story unfolded, live, only on Twitter. To start your twitterverse training, you might find a trending topic and contribute to the conversation.

Sometimes the conversation is random and unorganized, other times there may be an organizer present who sets a theme, or even a date and time for a group chat so that everyone can converse in real-time. If you're an expert, or just want to gather a group of like-minded people together in 140-character bursts of brilliance, you can just start a hashtag and make it happen.

One popular hashtag is #FF – Follow Friday — where Twitter users recommend to their followers other Twitter users to follow. The tweets look like this:

@missadventuring: #FF My adventurous motorcycle gal pals @advgoddess @fuzzygalore @overlandexpo @trilliumliz @madsocial @ruggedrider @daiquiric

Read this great piece in the NY Times titled In Praise of the Hashtag (http://nyti.ms/11FsROh).

Just to clarify terms: You use Twitter to tweet. Where do you tweet? On the Twitter web page, which is linear and rather #awkward, so either use the TweetDeck desktop and smartphone app, or HootSuite, a browser-based app, to #organize your tweets and Twitter feeds. Both tools will let you tweet to multiple accounts, and even to your Facebook and LinkedIn status updates.

LinkedIn

The best place for non-fiction and business authors to be is LinkedIn, where you can reach large groups of people who are working in your niche or industry. Because you're an expert, you can answer questions and provide how-to information for people searching for advice. This can lead directly to book sales, even bulk book sales to entire departments who really do need the information you've written about.

LinkedIn gets you "connections," not "friends," and many people carefully vet their connections, not accepting every invitation. If you've met someone at a conference, heard them speak or have used their product, make sure to mention that in your invitation to connect with them.

Make sure to join some groups, contribute, and stick with them for a while. Don't market yourself yet. Just give people the thumbs up for their contributions, where deserved, while you get familiar with the LinkedIn vibe. Professional groups are much more picky and critical than social groups.

Your profile on LinkedIn should be as well-written as a resume. Every group has a Discussions tab where you can start or contribute to a conversation. There's a Promotions tab where you can post information about your upcoming seminars, your book press releases, awards and information about articles you have written. You can recommend people you've worked with — which almost always gets you a reciprocal recommendation. And you can endorse people you know for their skills. Your behavior here should be as formal and polite as the offices you work in. Who knows. You may not only get more book sales, but be offered the job of your dreams.

Mailing Lists

Mailing lists are the most overlooked social media marketing. However anyone gets to your website — a google search, a business card, a web link — they're there because they're interested in you and what you're doing. They click, they see, and they think, "Hmmmm. Interesting." But there's no mailing list signup form, so they're gone.

Don't lose them. Use MailChimp, Constant Contact, Vertical Response, AWeber or another service to create your list, and put the widget on your web pages. Most have introductory prices of $0 up to a certain number of subscribers. Don't feel obligated to send out a newsletter until you have something to say. You can let them know about excerpts you've put up on Wattpad, or a guest blog post, or let them know about your Facebook Like page.

Widgets

A lot of social tools provide widgets that you can embed directly into your website. Most of us are familiar with Facebook widgets such as the "Like" button or box. And we've seen a lot of Twitter widgets, too, like "share a link", "feed" and "retweet." WattPad's widget shows off your stories and readers there. Scribd has several widgets (*scribble*, *readcast* and *share* collections).

Where will people go to read you? Look around for community sites that attract you, and try them out by posting a story and finding other authors stories to read and comment on. And always remember, people follow people, not books or businesses. It's a conversation.

Hiring it Out?

Sound like too much work? Please don't be sucked in by author services packages that advertise promotion and marketing services, including social media setup and coaching, that cost between $1,500 and $15,000. Karen Leland, a San Francisco Bay Area book publicist and president of Sterling Marketing Group, says that clients often come to her on the verge of tears after paying an exorbitant amount of money for just one press release sent to traditional media channels, with no results.

"While the best publicist in the world can't guarantee which publication, blog, radio or TV show will run with a review of an author's book, or interview them as an expert, there are certain things a dedicated publicist can do to customize the PR campaign and improve the odds the writer will get picked up by media," she said. "The problem with the generic approach author services companies take is that it's 'one size fits all.' That rarely produces the best results."

If you're going to hire a publicist, Leland recommends that you request a detailed plan that includes the specific projects that will be part of the campaign, the timeline for delivering on these projects, what you as the author are expected to provide to the publicist, and the process by which the publicist will keep you updated on the progress of your campaign. And be sure to ask them to provide other authors as references.

What does all this marketing get you? More money! In the next chapter you'll find out where and how you can sell your book.

10

Where's the Money? Royalties, Fees and Stores

One reason digital book sales are so popular with self-publishers is that the profit margin is very high. There are many ways to sell print books and e-books and the associated fees and royalties vary wildly. Use one method or a combination for the best combination of profit and distribution.

- Sell digital downloads from your own online store to earn 100% of sales minus operating expenses
- Employ an e-book aggregator/distributor
- Upload your e-book individually to each online retailer

This chapter provides an overview of fees and royalties for popular services, based on US dollars, though all of these services cross borders so you can sell internationally.

Your Own Online Store

Most self-publishers rely on distribution services to sell their books, but the most profitable place to sell is on your own website. You can use a e-commerce website builder like Yola, HostBaby or Shopify to sell digital downloads and physical books. If you like WordPress, integrate one of the many store plugins to sell direct. New options are popping up all the time, like the relatively new GumRoad service. Let's take a look at some example services so you know what's reasonable when you're looking around.

GumRoad is on my short list of recommended services. It's a hosting, payment and delivery service for digital content. You upload your digital file to a URL (your blog, website or FTP site), or upload the file to their site (maximum file size limit of 4GB, per product). Sell your electronic books, songs, movies, games, even software. They take 5% plus 25 cents for each transaction and pay every other Friday for all sales up to a week before that date, if you've made at least $10. I just can't wait until they have a product that integrates into my website.

LeanPub is also on my short list. It's a publishing system and a store, all in one. It's free to create your book, and you earn 90% minus 50 cents per sale.

PayPal for Digital Goods lets you sell digital files and even subscriptions for a 2.9% fee on net sales plus a $0.30 transaction fee. You'll probably need to hire a web professional to integrate this into your website. The money goes into your account immediately upon sale.

HostBaby is a website builder associated with self-publishing service BookBaby (also FilmBaby, CDBaby) that provides a website solution for writers and artists for $20. Their ListBaby newsletter service — competitive with Constant Contact, MailChimp, AWeber, and other mailing list services — comes free with a HostBaby account.

Shopify is just one of many popular e-commerce website builders easy enough to build yourself. They offer a range of packages starting at $29 per month. You can sell both digital and physical product with 0%-2% transaction fees depending on the level of your website plan. Payment is immediate upon sale.

Distribution Services and Aggregators

There are several advantages to working with aggregators (for e-books) and distribution services (for print books) instead of working directly with individual online e-book retailers:

- upload once, distribute everywhere for about 15% on sales
- centralized accounting
- better rates with retailers

Smashwords pays authors an 85% royalty when your book sells in their store and 60%, more or less, when they sell your book via a retailer (like B&N, Apple, etc.). They pay 30-40 days after the quarter ends.

BookBaby charges from $99 to about $300 to set up the average book, and has no store of its own. Because they make their money upfront, they don't take a cut of your royalties. When your book is sold through their distribution service via an online retailer (B&N, Apple, Amazon, etc.) you are paid their royalty rate, anywhere from 70% to 50%. They pay immediately upon sale. **PressBooks** partners with BookBaby for distribution.

Vook, like Smashwords, takes 15% of sales in their store with an additional 30% if sold through Apple, 50% with B&N, and 56.8% via Amazon. Their eCommerce platform Stripe takes 2.9% and charges a $0.30 per transaction fee.

Aerbook Maker plans to add a distribution service, but as of this writing, you must distribute your books directly to retailers. Their service is free but when you want to download and distribute your book, you pay what they call "export credits" — $29 for one or $99 for five. Use one credit for each e-book format: EPUB, Kindle, iBooks fixed layout, HTML5 for the web, etc.

PigeonLab distributes and handles accounting for your e-books for a 10% fee. You deliver the files — created from Aerbook Maker, InDesign, PressBooks Scrivener, Folium Studio or any of their recommended e-book creation services. They send you quarterly payments by check or PayPal.

Online Retailers

If you prefer, you can upload directly to each individual e-book retailer and manage each relationship separately. Here are a few examples of royalties.

Amazon KDP pays authors a 70% royalty on books priced between $2.99 – $9.99. On books outside that price range, your royalty is far smaller at 35%. So you would make more money on a Kindle e-book priced $5.99 than you would for one priced at $10.99. If Amazon discovers that you are selling your e-book for any less, anywhere on the web, including on your own website, it will automatically match that price. Which is why the coupon codes, like the ones offered on Smashwords, are so handy. Barnes & Noble, like Amazon, pays 65%

for books priced between $2.99 and $9.99, and only 40% on books outside that range.

Kobo pays 70% for books priced between 2.99 and 12.99 and 45% for books outside that range. Like Amazon, if they find that your book is selling anywhere else for a lower price, they can elect to match that price and pay your royalties based on that price.

Apple pays 70% of sales in the iBookstore.

For print books, use CreateSpace to create and sell via the Amazon store, and make sure to choose Expanded Distribution Channel (EDC) to get your print book into other online retailers like Ingram Group's Lightning Source, Baker & Taylor, and Barnes & Noble.

E-Book Royalties for Traditionally Published Authors

One of the reasons many traditionally published authors jumped ship was because their publishers were paying them the same royalty rate for e-books as they were for print books. This gaffe cost traditional publishing many good authors and also a lawsuit for price fixing. But the Titanic is turning, and now giving authors a more fair rate for e-books sold. What's a good rate? The best discussion on this topic I've seen so far is Kelly McClymer's blog post "How Much Should an Author's Ebook Royalty Be? Number Crunching Ahead" (http://bit.ly/ 13xPSkb, with a nod to her scientist and math whiz husband). And the number is... drumroll...42 (nodding to Douglas Adams). The number, after much promised crunching and explanation, "should be between 31.4% and 45% of net."

Libraries

Smashwords Library Direct complements Smashwords' existing relationships with library aggregators such as Baker & Taylor's Axis 360 and 3M's Cloud Library. The service is targeted to the small subset of libraries who want to host and manage their own e-books.

Kindle Lending Library

If you're enrolled in Amazon's exclusive KDP Select program you are participating in the **Kindle Lending Library**. Every month, Amazon sets a budget for how much they'll pay authors who participate and the royalties are split among the allocated budget. They explain it like this: if the budget is $600,000, and 600,000 prime users check out books during the month, an author would get $1 for every one of their books was checked out. If only 300,000 prime members check out books, the author would get $2 per book. When you enroll in the KDP Select program you can't sell your book anywhere else, but they market books in this program so well that your book may experience a great publicity boost and subsequent sales. Many authors find that launching their book with KDP Select, and then distributing elsewhere, is a good marketing strategy.

When Do You Get Paid?

Payment schedules do change, so check before you sign up, especially if you're concerned about cash flow. Terms range from royalties paid by check 30-60 days after the quarter ends (Smashwords and Vook) to when you've made at least $10 (by electronic payment) or $100 (by check), to immediately upon sale (BookBaby). Many companies can pay you by direct deposit to your bank account or PayPal email address.

11

How to Copyright Your Work

With the perceived risk among writers of copyright infringement so extremely high, it's no wonder self-publishers are increasingly concerned about making sure their work is copyrighted. The key word in the previous sentence is "perceived." Self-publishers worry too much about copyright, spending valuable time and money on assuring it instead of on writing and marketing.

In reality, you probably do not need to register a copyright. U.S. copyright law (and similar laws in many other countries) states that copyright exists from the moment the work is created, "without any action taken by the author, the moment it is fixed in a tangible form so that it is perceptible either directly or with the aid of a machine or device." That means that your words are yours, whether it's in your book, your blog, a speech or any other media.

You don't even have to put a copyright notice on your work, though it may ward off potential word thieves. You will have to register, however, if you wish to bring a lawsuit for infringement of a U.S. work.

A better reason to copyright your book is to make it visible to the library market, because all works submitted are also reviewed by Library of Congress selection librarians. That doesn't necessarily mean that a library will buy your book, but you can see if it has been catalogued by searching http://catalog.loc.gov. (You can also work with a professional librarian at a local library to obtain library cataloging.)

Many self-publishing service companies now offer copyright services, but you don't need to use them. While they charge up to $150 for the service, it costs only $35 to easily do it yourself. You can also register works of visual arts, performing arts, sound recordings and single serials. It takes the Copyright Office about 3 months to process electronic filings, and 10 months (plus $65) to process paper filings. Below is the short version of a detailed step-by-step procedure that includes screenshots published on PBS MediaShift in 2012 (see: http://to.pbs.org/16h0c3r).

> 1. To get started, point your browser to the US Government's official copyright registration page: http://www.copyright.gov/eco/.

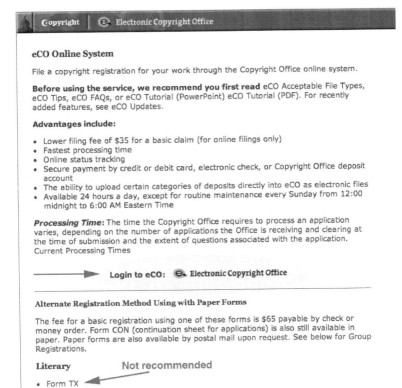

> 1. Now agree to their security and privacy notice and click **Continue to eCO to register a new claim.**
> 2. Fill out your personal information and register your work, providing details about your book. The system makes you complete each step in order, and from time to time, lets

you **Save For Later**. Once you've completed a step, or saved for later, you can click back and forth among the steps.

3. Authors will choose **Literary**, though if you have associated visual arts, music, videos or other works, you can copyright them separately using this system.

4. Enter your information as instructed on each screen and from the drop-down menus, using the Help screens when necessary. Make sure you've correctly entered your information and, if you make a mistake, use the pencil and trash icons at the far right of the screen as needed.

5. After you fill in the **Publication Completion** screen, the **Authors** screen will appear, then, after that, the **Claimants** form. Use the **Add Me** button to add yourself — the system will take your information from your registration information. Click **New** to add a different author.

6. The next screens to complete are the **Rights & Permissions** screen, the **Correspondent** screen, and the **Mail Certificate** form.

7. On the **Special Handling** form you'll see that a $760 fee discourages the choice. So unless you're in the middle of litigation or you're rich and impatient, just move on to the **Certification** form.

8. You're almost done now, and can check your work via the **Review Submission** form by clicking back through the screens you've filled out to make sure you've filled everything out correctly.

9. When everything's right, click the **Add to Cart** button to exit the eCO Copyright screenset and launch the payment system. You can pay with your checking account by clicking **Pay – Deposit Acct** or click **Pay – Credit Card / ACH** to use plastic.

10. Once you click the **Submit Payment** button at the bottom of the screen, you'll be taken back into the eCO Copyright screenset so you can upload your book. Though it is an option, registration by mail is not recommended as the government copyright office is so extremely overwhelmed. So click **Upload Deposit**.

11. The **Electronic Deposit Upload** screen lets you navigate to your computer hard drive and choose your book files. Upload your cover and interior file separately or all in one file.

Between the time you pay for your copyright registration, and three months from then, check your case status by logging in and clicking **All Cases** in the Check Registration Case Status menu at the left of the screen.

If you'd like a more detailed step-by-step with screenshots, please visit the PBS MediaShift article: http://to.pbs.org/16h0c3r.

Resources

> U.S. Government Copyright FAQ: http://www.copyright.gov/help/faq/faq-general.html

> Do you live in Canada? Here's their site: http://bit.ly/101VY8e

> Australians, look here: http://bit.ly/19uvfoM

> New Zealanders have similar rules: http://www.copyright.org.nz/viewFaq.php?faq=352

> In the UK, you'll go here: https://secure.copyrightservice.co.uk/register/reg_online.

12

Professional Print On Demand (POD) with Lightning Source

Lightning Source (LSI) is a publisher services company owned by Ingram, the largest book distributor in the world. Before Amazon's CreateSpace came along, self-publishers had to use LSI. But CreateSpace is an author services company that made print book creation and distribution a lot easier. Still, there are reasons you might want to use LSI instead, or in combination with other services.

Print Quality

The POD print quality from LSI is slightly better than that of other POD services:

- Most POD services give your book a thick glossy cover that looks like a cheap, shiny suit. LSI gives you better-looking glossy covers, and also offers matte covers, which look a lot better on many books.
- Most POD services have sloppier tolerances. A 1/8-inch tolerance, which is acceptable for many, means that your spine might wrap over onto your back or front cover, just a little bit. LSI's tolerances are higher.
- LSI's creme interior is also much better looking. It's actually creme and not the yellow you see with some POD books.
- With LSI, the ink is truly black, where other POD services can have grayish printing, as if they're watering down the ink.

Distribution

Because LSI is owned by Ingram, your book will automatically be visible to bookstores. But then, so are books created with CreateSpace as long as you use their Expanded Distribution Channel. LSI charges a $75 setup fee. CreateSpace only charges $25 for the expanded distribution.

If you find yourself becoming a small press, you may want to use LSI's offset and short-run printing services, POD, and e-book distribution. They also offer a returns program which, in combination with a 55% discount, is the only way bookstores will be remotely tempted to stock your book on their shelves.

LSI can also distribute your EPUB, PDF, LIT and EREADER e-book files through their Ingram Digital partner. However, other services recommended in this book are much simpler and easier to work with.

Fees

Costs are fuzzy with a lot of subsidy presses. You may end up paying as much or more than you spend with LSI for its "free" setup, by buying its pro and expanded distribution plans, editing and design services, and returns programs. Also remember that the author services companies often make money by marking up the per-book print price.

- It costs $75 to set up a title with LSI, and they charge a $40 file manipulation fee to upload revisions. That kind of pricing has been an industry standard forever, and it seems non-competitive in these days of free and really cheap. But my theory is that they don't want to deal with the glut of self-publishers who don't know what they're doing. And if you've hired a professional designer (yes, you should), and have used CreateSpace to get cheap proofs, you really shouldn't need to revise.
- LSI charges $30 for proofs, plus shipping and handling, whereas CreateSpace charges the per-book cost and postage.
- LSI's price per-book is slightly higher, but when you look at the quality side-by-side, you might agree that it's worth it.

- Lightning Source is used to working with experts, and the reps don't respond as immediately or as patiently as customer service for CreateSpace, for example.

Using LSI in Combination with Other Services

If you want to use LSI to print and distribute, you'll probably want to take advantage of these other services, too:

1. Use CreateSpace to print your proofs. They only charge printing costs and postage to send you a book, while Lightning Source charges $45 for print proofs.

2. Then when the book is perfect, join the CreateSpace Pro Plan and let them supply Amazon.com. They'll never go out of stock on Amazon (because they own CreateSpace), whereas sometimes when you set up a channel from another supplier you can get the dreaded "Available in 2 or 3 Weeks" label on your book page.

3. Pay $75 to Lightning Source to set up your book and let them supply it to other print book retailers. If you really want brick-and-mortar stores to stock your book, make sure your discount is 55% and make it returnable.

4. When your print book is perfect, you have a few choices for e-book creation and distribution. You can let CreateSpace create a Kindle version of your print book for $65. When you get the file, upload it via the Kindle Direct Publishing (KDP) program. Then make a copy of the KDP file, assign a different ISBN, and make other changes as required to publish with Smashwords. This will get your book into all the other e-book retailers and app stores and make it available to libraries. Alternately, hire BookBaby or Vook to create and distribute your e-book for $99, handing over all the distribution to them, including to Amazon Kindle, Sony, Apple, B&N and Kobo. Or you can create your e-book using Folium Studio, Scrivener, PressBooks and other tools recommended in this book.

Book Cover Templates

Maybe you've hired a professional designer who is using InDesign or Quark to lay out your book. Or maybe you've bought InDesign, and are trying to learn it yourself. (Aaarg! But it can be worth it if you're planning a series of books.) LSI provides free book cover templates for all the standard book sizes. You (or your designer) don't even have to register or sign in. Just navigate to LightningSource.com's *File Creation* area, click *Cover Template Creation*, and tick off the options that fit your book. Finally, enter your email address and, seconds later, you'll get the cover template in your email.

Weight and Spine-Width Calculator

The spine width in your book cover template only works if you're printing with LSI because of differences in paper weight among all the various printers. So if you're printing elsewhere, you'll have to adjust the spine width to match their specifications. (They all have spine-width calculators.) If you have trouble adjusting your spine width in a program like InDesign, take a Lynda.com course for the program or, better yet, there are plenty of professionals who can help you, for a small fee.

Bar Codes

A bar code costs about $25, but your LSI book cover template will include a bar code for free! If you've entered your ISBN (buy it from Bowker), and the price of your book, that information will also be embedded in the bar code. Don't worry, if you haven't decided, you don't have to fill in the ISBN or price in order to get a cover template. You can do it later, before you actually print your book. Once you're ready, just generate another template, copy the bar code art, and paste it into your designed cover.

13

New Self-Publishing Tools Even Change the Way We Write

Today's tools marry writing and publishing, bringing artists ever closer to the end product with click-of-a-button e-book creation capabilities built into the writing tools themselves. Devices allow the very definition of a book to change, now that a work no longer has to fit inside a particular size of binding.

I've been using Scrivener, a tool developer Keith Blount created to help outline, edit and storyboard his own novel. In an interview by Mac AppStorm, he explains that "I kept thinking that there must be a better software solution [than MS Word] for this way of working, something that would allow me to rearrange a long document using synopses, to allow me to edit the text in small pieces or as a whole and so on."

Scrivener allows authors to write, organize, and "grow" books, scripts, even articles. Converting the document to an e-book, web page, a PDF for print or a Word doc works surprisingly well, with just a few clicks.

Scrivener is the first significant software tool that has truly changed the way writers create books since MS Word, an application that we love or hate but that is undeniably embedded in business culture, writing culture, and anybody-who-wants-to-write-a-letter culture. Word has become so easy to use that even professional writers, who consider it their primary tool, often create really sloppy documents with it. In my self-publishing workshops, I am constantly amazed that professional writers have not troubled themselves to learn the intricacies of their most important tool, especially using "styles" to automatically format titles, headings and paragraphs (at the very least).

Microsoft Word is Still Very Important

Learning Word styles may never have really mattered, except Mark Coker built the Smashwords "meatgrinder" conversion tool around MS Word styles. (Amazon Kindle Direct Publishing relies on consistent document styles, too.) If a writer does not know how to wield styles, he or she will simply not be able to successfully upload the book for distribution to e-book retailers.

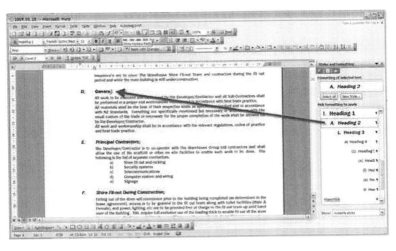

Smashwords was founded in 2008. In its first year, it published 140 books from 90 authors. Its catalog reached 6,000 books in 2009,

28,800 in 2010, 92,000 in 2011, and in 2012 it has more than 140,000 books, many from first-time authors. Why? Ease of publication. But the general concept of a book has remained the same — a written or illustrated work with a certain number of printed pages, and an e-book as the same book, but delivered electronically, possibly containing hyperlinks to the web.

But with authors no longer looking to traditional publishing to define terms, a book no longer must hold a certain number of words or pages to be printed on the "signatures" that get fed through a printing press. No longer does it even have to be on paper. How many pages is a book, anyway — 26 pages, 2,600 pages, 26,000? Authors are just beginning to realize that we can include not only hyperlinks, but audio, video, voiceovers, animations and even physics that allow interactive gameplay. When do we stop thinking of our book as just a book, and start thinking about hybrid publications, such as book and "website," "app" or "game?"

Crossing into the Game Space

Picture and multimedia toolmakers naturally cross these boundaries. Alex Souza, who developed the Kwik Photoshop plug-in, is thrilled that a book can expand into game territory, but realizes that this can be intimidating for some. "Authors can expand their stories with features not available in the traditional media, and creating for digital devices requires a new set of skills," Souza said. "Creating a multimedia e-book that expands into game territory requires the author to think about the entire experience: audio, visual, even tactile. While this excites many, the increased complexity frightens others. So my goal for Kwik is to remove as much of the learning curve as possible, leaving them free to do their best, which is transform ideas into magic."

Marrying Words with Multimedia

Matthew Cavnar, president of Vook, the popular multimedia e-book creation service, said, "I've seen authors change their vision when they became aware of how the e-book medium allowed them to expand their story or narrative or the message outside of their book ... It might seem like a small thing, but putting a link into a book connects that book to the Internet, and by extension every idea and thing and community that people have created digitally."

Cavnar cites Jeff Corwin, the nature conservationist and television personality, as an example. "He knew he wanted to expand his message into books, and when he and his team realized they could add video, they understood that they could now represent that core part of Jeff's identity as a television personage within the book format itself." The writers on Jeff's team were able to create a multimedia book, instead of separate media properties for book, app, audio and video.

Small Publishing Innovates Faster

But these new tech tools are not just for self-publishers anymore. While you don't see Big Publishing innovating much around the new capabilities, smaller publishers are eager to be first in the space. Remember the popup book? They were mostly for kids, but I remember some great artsy books that used the delightful and complex popup "technology." Unicorn Labs, a developer of e-books and early learning apps, worked with popup book maker David A. Carter to create "Spot the Dot," delivered through iTunes. Chief Product Officer Mark Sigal describes it as "an interactive picture book app comprised of 10 different playspaces for young minds, such as 'Sliding Windows,' 'Popcorn' and 'Spinning Coins.' We worked with the author to rethink the medium of the popup book for the iPad, a domain where touch, tilt, drag and rich voice and sound are native to the 'canvas.'" Kirkus Book Reviews recognized "Spot the Dot" as one of the Best Kids' Book Apps of 2011.

Marketing Gets Integrated into the Writing Process

New services not only break through authors' ideas of what a book is, but help them market the book too, with built-in book publicity tools. "The idea that the book you build can be simultaneously integrated with the fabric of the social web leads to the book as a centerpiece for conversation leading to discovery and sales," said Ron Martinez, founder of Aerbook Maker, a multimedia picture e-book creation tool in the cloud that publishes for EPUB, KF8, HTML5, iOS and Android.

While authors are creating, they can also be marketing by publishing their books "in whole or in part to the web, with pages shareable on Twitter, Pinterest, Facebook and other social networks," Martinez said. Aerbook authors can embed "share" buttons in their e-books. One nifty feature even lets potential customers download a sample via SMS to your smartphone.

Blogs are also a great marketing tool, and a natural outlet for a writer's creativity. The very nature of blogging has also changed how many people write, in short or long bursts, in a casual, personal style. But why not build a book by blogging? The idea of blog-to-book systems have been around for a few years now. But the only success with blog-to-book making that actually works is PressBooks, which is the tool we've used to create this book you're reading now. Export your WordPress blog (or just the posts in a single category), import it into PressBooks, and you've got a draft. Slap on an introduction, a table of contents, a cover, and get it edited, and voila. You've got a book that can be delivered in formats ready for any of the e-readers and apps, for the web, and in PDF for print books.

Founder Hugh McGuire points out that the blog-to-book feature is only a small perk of of what he describes as "an online book publishing tool that happens to be built on top of open source blogging software, and we're used by well-known publishers such as Harvard Business Review Press, as well as upstarts like The Rogue Reader... not to convert blogs into books, but rather to produce books." He adds that "The thing we do that few others do is produce e-books, typeset PDFs for print on demand, and produce web versions (public or private) of every book." They can also run publisher catalogs. For an example, see the AskMen catalog. For e-book distribution to Kindle, Apple iBooks and other retailers, they partner with BookBaby.

Kevin Gao of Hyperink, an e-book publisher that seeks experts and works with bloggers (like Penelope Trunk) "to curate their existing posts, videos, and comments and create books," said that "technology enables authors to think beyond just a book towards things like the backend channel, for example, using the book to promote more expensive products like videos, conferences and follow-up books. While books build your brand and customer base, higher-priced products are where an author can make serious money." Gao pointed out that really savvy authors see books "as just the starting point in building a larger personal, digital, online brand now. No longer are books an end point in themselves," said Gao, "but just one step in a funnel to build a community and monetize it."

Does All this Corrupt the Writing Process?

While purists might argue that merging marketing tools with writing tools corrupts the art of writing, remember that most authors have beta readers. They have traditionally been their editors, who critique and shape a work on behalf of the publisher and future book buyers, essentially pre-vetting the book for marketing. Today, in the absence of traditional publishing to shepherd writers, beta readers can be found on fan fiction sites, where "Fifty Shades of Grey" was shepherded into a knockout bestseller, and on social publishing sites like Wattpad (which is reaching beyond its young adult writers to literary, non-fiction and other genres), All Romance (if you're writing romance, you must be here), and Scribd (a document-sharing site that has great features for authors), to name a few.

One Author's Successful Experiment

Dorothee Kocks is an author who re-envisioned her book when she discovered the technical possibilities. She said, "I wanted to help create a conversation about the first American sexual revolution, in part because readers of my novel, 'The Glass Harmonica,' could then see the real history behind the 'Johnny Appleseed of porn' character in the book."

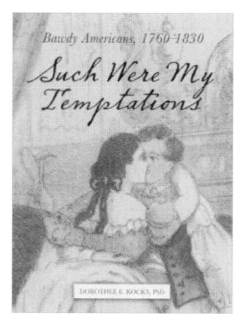

Kocks, who has a Ph.D. in American Studies from Brown University, authored a well-respected scholarly book and climbed the tenure ladder at the University of Utah before trying her hand, successfully, at historical fiction. But history remains her passion.

"I had already looked into enhanced e-books because they could showcase the erotic art so well from this period," said Knoks, "plus include videos like an actress reciting a bawdy poem from the 1760s ... Then it occurred to me that the book could be the conversation." The resulting multimedia book, produced and published with Aerbook Maker, is "Such Were My Temptations."

The book invites readers to respond to questions like "Is this porn?" and "Should we talk about our founding fathers' sex lives?" It links directly to an online salon. "Re-imagining the book as a conversation connected the project directly to what matters most – using history to help us become better people," said Kocks. Kocks talks about the project in this YouTube video.

Kocks told me in a December 5 email exchange, "The heart of the book is at the heart of Aerbook's design," which allows people to share pages from the preview on Aerbook, or by texting *tempt* to 415-944-4115. "The SMS text option was a surprise Ron [Martinez] sprung on me just yesterday, and a indicator of the hothouse creativity going on over there at Aerbook."

Links

- Scrivener, Literature & Latte - $45 per license, Mac and Windows, bulk licensing available. http://www.literatureandlatte.com/scrivener.php
- Aerbook Maker - Multimedia picture book maker – Free to play, $99 to export five formats (EPUB, Kindle, Android, etc.) for distribution. http://aerbook.com/
- Kwik -$249 Photoshop extension, a desktop app to create multimedia picture books. http://kwiksher.com/
- Vook - About $250 to create a multimedia e-book. http://vook.com/
- Hyperink - A publisher that helps experts and bloggers create e-books. http://hyperink.com/
- PressBooks - Free publishing tool and blog to book maker, with reasonably priced add-on services. http://pressbooks.com/
- Smashwords - Popular e-book creation and distribution service for text-heavy e-books. http://smashwords.com/
- Microsoft Word Style Basics (Video) http://bit.ly/16AkZyz

14

Literary Agents as Self-Publishing Consultants

With big publishing buying only the crème de la crème of books, and more authors turning to self-publishing, some savvy agents are acting as literary consultants to help their authors self-publish. This role offers up new opportunities and challenges for everybody in the industry. Three agents talk about their experiments to serve authors by widening their middle ground.

Ted Weinstein, a San Francisco-based agent who represents non-fiction authors, said that self-publishing "has added one more serious option for my clients when we are looking at all their possible opportunities." He's worked with authors he has successfully placed with traditional publishers "to launch additional mid-length material and backlisted books using new self-publishing tools." These tools include Amazon's CreateSpace and Kindle Direct Publishing, Barnes & Noble's PubIt, Smashwords and more.

Big publishing has not been set up to publish anything but books. Mid-length materials, worksheets and other writing that might be downloaded from Amazon or directly from the author's site are not in their repertoire. Neither do they help the author develop unpublished chapters into articles for placement in magazines. Though these kinds of supplemental materials help the author — and publisher — get attention and sales, the responsibility to create, distribute and publicize them lies with authors, many of whom turn to their agent.

Weinstein has long been interested in the struggle between traditional and self-publishing, and is fond of saying, "All publishing is self-publishing." His moderated online conversation with self-publishing phenom Amanda Hocking, who accepted a traditional publishing contract, and Barry Eisler, a traditionally published author moving to self-publishing, is a good place to start when trying to get a handle on the level of experimentation that's happening in the industry today. Also catch his Writers on Writing podcast interview archive dated September 2010 – and still very valid — on the topic of agents, e-books and self-publishing.

Laurie McLean, an agent with Larsen Pomada Literary Agents in San Francisco, spent more than 25 years in high-tech publicity and marketing before she started her career as a literary agent. McLean, who also co-organizes the San Francisco Writers Conference and runs SF Writers University, knows how to work the web and social media. Like Weinstein, she is "incorporating self-publishing into every one of my clients' career plans for backlist titles, experimental fiction, shorter works and more."

Laura Rennert, senior agent with the Andrea Brown Literary Agency, has taken it a step further, pioneering an indie-publishing path for the agency's authors. The first to debut is a young adult novel titled "Solstice" by P.J. Hoover, an author who previously published a series for younger readers with small press CBAY Books.

Rennert shopped "Solstice" to traditional publishers, and it even went to acquisitions at one house. She said that when it was finally rejected (because it was too similar to another book being published by a big name house), "we realized this was a concern we were likely going to run into elsewhere, so Hoover made the choice, in consultation with me, to go the independent publishing route and be the first to work with our agency in this capacity."

"We are not becoming a publisher," she said. "We're building slowly, figuring things out, and adapting to the changing market and to our authors' needs." The agency handles formatting, conversion, cover design, jacket copy, editing and proofreading, with the author in complete control. "We also aggressively shop all sub-rights, including foreign, audio and film/TV/performance," Rennert said.

Where's the Money?

It's an interesting paradigm shift — literary agency as publishing consultant — and there is no standard.

"I think we may be in our own bucket for the moment. We are not a packager or a publisher, and we are not acquiring or licensing rights from the author," Rennert said, in response to my observation that much of these services are provided by companies like Bookmasters. "We are not charging any fees ... Our only compensation after recouping our clearly defined costs [formatting/conversion, cover design, and proofreading] which are agreed upon upfront and which we pass through transparently, is our standard 15 percent commission."

So Hoover — "a fabulous self-promoter and a very talented author," Rennert said — earns back her debt to the agency, and the agency gets 15 percent to cover "the hours and months we devote to editorial; figuring out how to position and package the book to reach the right market; the time spent on quality control; seeking out and dealing with high-caliber vendors providing the above services; and locating and vetting professional photographers and cover designers whose work is every bit as good as those used in traditionally published books."

With the agency getting 15 percent, the author earns 85 percent. With this model, authors may soon be flocking to agencies for publishing instead of for representation to big publishers. Is the agent, formerly an ally, becoming the competition for publishers?

"The answer is that authors are driving this trend in publishing," Rennert said, "and it is my job as a literary agent to represent my author's interests ... My role is to help them navigate the publishing landscape and maximize their potential."

While Rennert's agency seems to have settled on a 15 percent commission, Weinstein is still working out various fee-based and royalty services for the myriad of projects his authors need. And McLean charges $500 for a litany of deliverables in her Agent Savant package.

Self-Publishing As Marketing Test

Today, self-publishing has lost its stigma, with agents and big publishers thinking of it as a market test. So for authors who dream of gaining an agent and a publishing house, don't worry that self-publishing will hurt your chances — though building a platform is essential. Hoover successfully self-published three previous books before Rennert took her latest project. Weinstein looks for platform and the ability to self-promote. If self-published authors sell more than 5,000–10,000 copies of their book, "at a minimum," he said, that gets his attention.

One of Weinstein's authors is Peter Montoya, who he placed with McGraw-Hill, and whose self-published book "The Brand Called You" sold 60,000 copies worldwide.

McLean found her first self-published author, Kait Nolan, by reading her comments on a blog. McLean was impressed by her advice. "So I went to Kait's blog (conveniently appended to each of her comments), read her free e-novella, paid 99 cents for the sequel, and by then I was hooked on her combined strengths of writing style, unique voice, mastery of social media and gutsy attitude. She also posted that she'd sold 1,000 copies of her 99-cent novella in the first month it was available, so I knew she was on top of the business end of things, too."

The Experiment Continues

For authors faced with choosing a DIY self-publishing package or starting their own small press (with the burden of fronting the expense of editorial and design), it's a clear win. But for the agent? It's too soon to tell. "It's a newer venture for us," Rennert said, "so success isn't yet proven."

These agents are right in the middle of the whirlwind, playing with various consulting services and fee structures to see what works. But they all share one quality: excitement about the ability to help their authors succeed by experimenting with new publishing tools and technologies, paying attention to this rapidly changing marketplace, and creating their own models while the industry nervously watches.

About the Author

Carla King has been writing for PBS MediaShift since 2010. She is an author, a publishing consultant, and founder of the Self-Publishing Boot

Camp program providing books, lectures and workshops for prospective self-publishers. She has self-published since 1994 and has worked in multimedia since 1996. Find her speaking schedule, workshops and her Self-Publishing Boot Camp Guide for Authors on SelfPubBootCamp.com.

29197168R00054

Made in the USA
Lexington, KY
17 January 2014